200 Years with Abraham Lincoln

One Man's Life and Legacy

Helen Koutras Bozonelis

Enslow Publishers, Inc.
40 Industrial Road
Box 398
Berkeley Heights, NJ 07922
USA

http://www.enslow.com

Library of Congress Cataloging-in-Publication Data

Bozonelis, Helen Koutras.
200 years with Abraham Lincoln : one man's life and legacy / Helen Koutras Bozonelis.
p. cm.
Includes bibliographical references and index.
Summary: "Read about Abraham Lincoln's life and his lasting impact on America and the world"—
Provided by publisher.
ISBN-13: 978-0-7660-3266-8
ISBN-10: 0-7660-3266-3
1. Lincoln, Abraham, 1809-1865—Juvenile literature. 2. Lincoln, Abraham, 1809-1865—Influence—
Juvenile literature. 3. Presidents—United States—Biography—Juvenile literature. I. Title. II. Title: Two
hundred years with Abraham Lincoln.
E457.905.B65 2008
973.7092—dc22
[B]   2007037243

Printed in the United States of America

10 9 8 7 6 5 4 3 2 1

To Our Readers:
We have done our best to make sure all Internet addresses in this book were active and appropriate when we went to press. However, the author and the publisher have no control over and assume no liability for the material available on those Internet sites or on other Web sites they may link to. Any comments or suggestions can be sent by e-mail to comments@enslow.com or to the address on the back cover.

♻ Enslow Publishers, Inc., is committed to printing our books on recycled paper. The paper in every book contains 10% to 30% post-consumer waste (PCW). The cover board on the outside of each book contains 100% PCW. Our goal is to do our part to help young people and the environment too!

Photo Credits: American Treasures of the Library of Congress, p. 39 (bottom right); Christopher Bruno/Sxc.hu, all headers unless otherwise noted; Courtesy of the Lincoln Museum, Fort Wayne, IN, pp. 7, 9; The Granger Collection, New York, pp. 4, 16, 38, 46; © istockphoto/Kevin Lloyd, p. 10; © istockphoto.com/Richard Gunion, p. 41; © 2008 Jupiterimages Corporation, p. 26; Library of Congress, Prints and Photographs Division, pp. 5, 8, 12, 13, 14–15, 17, 19, 20, 21, 23, 25, 27, 28, 29, 30, 31, 32, 33, 34 (top left) 36–37, 39, 43, 44–45, 49, 51 (top), 53, 57–64 ; Manuscript Division, Library of Congress, p. 6 and all backgrounds unless otherwise noted; National Museum of American History, Smithsonian Institution, pp. 1, 34 (bottom); Nicole DiMella, p. 54; Picture History, p. 51 (bottom); Shutterstock, p. 53 (bottom right); Sxc.hu, pp. 15, 18, 26, 31, 36, 40, 48, 51, 55; U.S. National Archives and Records Administration, p. 35

Cover Photos: Library of Congress, Prints and Photographs Division (spine photo); National Museum of American History; Shutterstock (back cover); Smithsonian Institution (tophat); Sxc.hu (flag); The Granger Collection, New York (Lincoln); U.S. National Archives and Records Administration (proclamation).

Lincoln

FROM "FOOL" TO HERO

Riots broke out in New York after Lincoln called for more men to fight in the Civil War.

Things were not going well for Lincoln. It was the summer of 1864, near the end of his first term as president. He wanted to be elected again. But he was the most hated politician America had ever known.

The nation was torn in two by the Civil War. Half the North wanted Lincoln out of office. In the South, people hanged and burned images of Lincoln. Newspapers called the president "a coward," "shattered, dazed, utterly foolish," "a mole-eyed monster," and worse.[1] They demanded that he resign. Lincoln was an unpopular president during an unpopular war.

Within less than a year, though, people in the United States—and around the world—would change from cursing Lincoln to praising him as a great American. Why is Lincoln still remembered as a hero almost two hundred years after his birth?

THE MAKING OF A PRESIDENT

Chapter 1

In a deep forest in Kentucky, on a farm called Sinking Spring, Abraham Lincoln was born on February 12, 1809. Abe's father Thomas tried to earn a living out of the farm. Abe's mother, Nancy Hanks Lincoln, loved to read Bible stories to her children. Abe had an older sister named Sarah. His younger brother, Thomas, died as a baby.

Two years later, the Lincolns moved ten miles to a one-room home on a better farm called Knob Creek. Abe spent his days caring for the animals and planting pumpkin seeds.

Indiana Wilderness

By the time Abe turned seven, his family moved to Little Pigeon Creek, near the Ohio River in Indiana. But sadness hit the Lincoln household when Mrs. Lincoln died two years later. Abe adored his mother and praised her: "All that I am or ever hope to be, I owe it to her."[1]

Abe sewed pages together to create his own math book.

Abe's father soon married Sarah Bush Johnston, a widow with three children. "When she came into Indiana, Abe and his sister were wild, ragged and dirty," his cousin said. "She soaped, rubbed, and washed the children clean, so that they looked pretty, neat, well, and clean . . . and the children once more looked human as their own good mother left them."[2]

Abe said that all his schooling "did not amount to one year." However, a childhood friend remembered, ". . . he soared above us. He naturally assumed the leadership of the boys. He read & thoroughly read his books whilst we played. Hence he was above us and became our guide and leader."[3]

Leaving Home

From the age of fourteen, Abe worked away from home, but gave all his earnings to his father. Some of his jobs included splitting logs and working as a ferryman on the Ohio River. When his family moved to Illinois, he left home to be on his own. He was twenty-two years old.

Abe learned to make fence rails by splitting logs with an axe. By the time he was fourteen, Abe was already six feet tall and very athletic.

"Honest Abe"

Chapter 2

For the next ten years, Lincoln tried his hand at all sorts of jobs: store clerk, blacksmith, surveyor, postmaster, lawyer, merchant, soldier, and politician.[1] Eventually he found a job as a clerk in a general store in New Salem, Illinois. Before too long, Lincoln made friends because he was a natural-born storyteller and loved to tell jokes.

Captain Lincoln

Lincoln joined the army and left to fight Indians in the Black Hawk War. Within a few weeks, the soldiers made him their captain. This was one of the proudest moments of his life. Lincoln said this honor "gave me more pleasure than any I have had since."[2] He served

a total of ninety days, did not see any fighting, and received $124 for it.

A Self-Made Man

Lincoln returned to Salem after the war. He opened a store with a man named William Berry, but it failed within a few months. Berry died two years

Did You Know?

Lincoln's favorite sport was wrestling. His hobbies were memorizing poetry and going to the theater.

later, owing about $1,100 to many different peo- ple. Lincoln worked very hard to repay the debt, since he had been Berry's partner. It took fifteen years. People called him "Honest Abe."

Friends wanted him to enter politics. But Lincoln felt he had to improve himself first. On his own, he studied everything from English grammar to geometry. He borrowed law books and studied them late into the night after working all day. He became a lawyer on March 1, 1837.

"Get the books, and read and study them," was his advice. "Always bear in mind that your own resolution to succeed is more important than any other one thing."[3]

Springfield

Lincoln became a member of the Whig party and a state assemblyman. In 1837, he moved to the state capital in Springfield, Illinois, where there were more opportunities. He became a junior partner in a busy law firm and was elected to the state legislature.

During his twenty-four years in Springfield, Lincoln became a successful lawyer and politician.

Mary Todd Lincoln went to the White House with high hopes. But she suffered through many tragedies, including the deaths of three of her four sons and the assassination of her husband.

MARRYING MISS MARY

Abraham Lincoln fell in love with Miss Mary Todd, a wealthy young woman who also happened to be from Kentucky. He spotted her at a dance in Springfield and told her he wanted to dance with her "in the worst way." Later she joked with her cousin that "he certainly did."[1]

They were opposites who were attracted to each other. Lincoln was born ten years before Mary. He was tall and thin; she was short and plump. He grew up in a one-room log cabin; she in a fourteen-room mansion. He had little schooling; she went to boarding school for ten years. He was even-tempered; she was temperamental. He was somber; she was

lively. He kept his wilderness ways; she had social graces. But she was a match for his sharp tongue.

After a stormy courtship, they eventually married on November 4, 1842. He gave her a wedding ring, which he engraved with

Mary and Abraham Lincoln with three of their sons. Left to right: William, Robert, and Thomas ("Tad").

14

"Love is Eternal." They were devoted to each other. They were equally ambitious. Both loved politics and both wanted to live in the White House.[2]

Family Album

Abe and Mary had four sons whom they adored. Lincoln roughhoused with the boys and did not believe in disciplining them. Only Robert, their firstborn, lived to be an adult. Their three other sons died young. Edward died when he was three. William died in the White House when he was eleven. Thomas died when he was eighteen.

Abraham Lincoln
Defending young Armstrong

A RISING STAR

Chapter 4

Eventually Lincoln opened up his own law firm in downtown Springfield, with his friend William Herndon. Over the next fifteen years, Lincoln handled thousands of cases. He was often away on business for several months each year, while Mrs. Lincoln was at home raising the boys. Lincoln's reputation for fairness helped his career blossom. The backwoods farm boy from Kentucky was a rising star in Illinois.

Lincoln-Douglas Debates

Friends urged Lincoln to run for Congress. He agreed to run for the United States Senate for the newly

Lincoln Links to Today

In 1860 Lincoln and Douglas ran against each other again—for the presidency. Lincoln did not campaign for himself. He gave no speeches, nor did he make public appearances. His supporters campaigned for him.

Now candidates can reach millions of voters. They appear on television and the Internet in ads and debates. However, the costs of using the media have skyrocketed and candidates have the burden of raising millions of dollars.

formed Republican party. In 1858, he ran against Stephen A. Douglas, the most powerful man in the Senate.

Lincoln made a speech that many thought stirred up trouble between the North and South. He spoke about keeping the United States together:

> A House divided against itself cannot stand. I believe this government cannot endure, permanently half slave and half free. I do not expect the Union to be dissolved—I do not expect the house to fall—but I do expect it will cease to be divided. It will become all one thing or all the other."[1]

18

Lincoln challenged Douglas to seven debates on slavery. Each one lasted three hours and drew noisy crowds of tens of thousands of people.

Lincoln promised to let slavery exist in the southern states, but to stop the spread of slavery in the territories. Douglas, a Democrat, believed each state should decide whether or not to allow it.

Douglas won the election, but the debates made Lincoln famous all across the nation.

Stephen Douglas was Lincoln's opposite in almost everything. Douglas was short and stout with a ruddy complexion, and had a booming voice. Lincoln was tall, painfully thin, and spoke in a high-pitched voice.

SLAVERY

By 1860 the United States was made up of 34 states. Differences between the Northern states and the Southern states tore apart the two regions.

About 22 million people lived in the North. About 9 million lived in the South—4 million of them were slaves.

The North was industrial with big cities. Most Northerners at the time felt slavery was cruel and evil. They said it was against liberty and equality. They called

This newspaper page from June 27, 1857, shows Dred Scott along with his wife (right) and daughters (top). The Dred Scott Supreme Court Case was a major turning point leading up to the Civil War.

themselves abolitionists and wanted slavery to be illegal in every state.

The South was agricultural with big farms and plantations that needed slave labor. Many Southerners felt slavery was not wrong and that Lincoln was their enemy.

One issue was whether slavery would be allowed in western territories that would come into the Union as states. The South warned that if Lincoln became president, they would leave the Union.

Slaves provided much of the labor that the Southern plantations required.

Dred Scott Decision

In 1857, the United States Supreme Court had heard a case called *Dred Scott v. Sanford*. Dred Scott was a slave who had moved with his master from Missouri, a slave state, to Illinois, a free state. When his master died, Scott sued to be a free man because he had been taken to an area that banned slavery.

The Supreme Court disagreed. It said Scott was not a citizen so he had no rights; he was property and belonged to his master. The decision was a setback for abolitionists, and a victory for the South. It also allowed slavery to spread in all the territories. Lincoln attacked the decision. He said the Declaration of Independence and the Constitution were intended to include blacks.[1]

Who Was John Brown?

John Brown hoped to start a revolution to free slaves throughout the South. Brown led a raid on the government armory at Harper's Ferry, Virginia, in 1859. He planned to give the guns to slaves who had escaped.

While Brown and his gang captured the armory, they were unable to defeat the United States Marines sent to stop them. Brown was captured and hanged. He became

Abolitionist John Brown has been called a martyr and a madman. His raid increased tensions that helped lead to the Civil War.

a hero to abolitionists. Lincoln said Brown showed "great courage" but "that cannot excuse violence, bloodshed, and treason."[2] Brown became a legend and people still sing about "John Brown's Body." But Southerners were afraid that there would be more slave revolts.

HAIL TO THE CHIEF

Chapter 6

Abraham Lincoln did not begin what would be the great work of his life until he was fifty-one years old. That is when he was elected President of the United States (POTUS), in November 1860.

The Lincoln family packed up and left Springfield for the White House on February 11, 1861. More than a thousand well-wishers came to see him off at the train station. He said a touching goodbye to his hometown friends:

> Here I have lived a quarter of a century and have passed from a young to an old man. Here my children have been born and one is buried. I now leave, not knowing when, or whether ever, I may return, with a task before me greater than that which rested about [George] Washington. . . . Without the assistance of that Divine Being who ever attended him, I cannot succeed. With that assistance I cannot fail.[1]

On March 4, 1861, Abraham Lincoln took the oath of office as the sixteenth President of the United States. Hannibal Hamlin, a senator from Maine, was Lincoln's vice-president. In his inaugural address, Lincoln pleaded with his "dissatisfied fellow countrymen" to avoid war. "We are not enemies, but friends. We must not be enemies."[2]

It was time for Lincoln to make history.

Did You Know?

Abraham Lincoln is the only president to have a patent. Patent 6469, dated March 10, 1849, was for a machine that he invented that would refloat boats that had run aground.

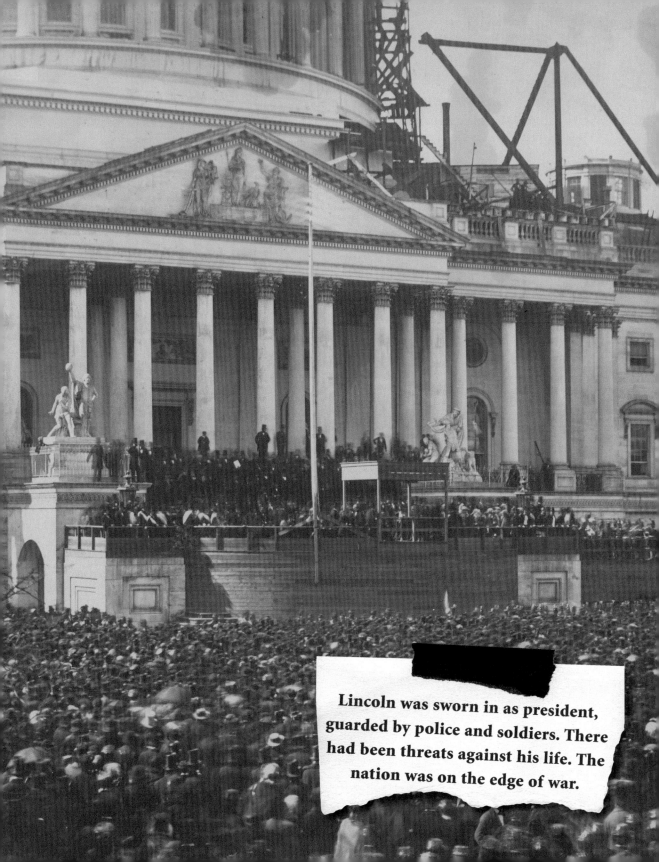

Lincoln was sworn in as president, guarded by police and soldiers. There had been threats against his life. The nation was on the edge of war.

President Lincoln visited the Antietam battlefield. Here, he is photographed with Allan Pinkerton (left) and General John A. McClernand.

MR. LINCOLN'S WAR

Chapter 7

Seven southern states seceded from the United States when Lincoln was elected president. These included South Carolina, Mississippi, Florida, Alabama, Georgia, Louisiana, and Texas. They formed their own separate country and called it the Confederate States of America.

Lincoln did not want to use force, but he believed that slavery should not spread into the free western territories. He also believed that no state had the right to leave the Union. In a letter to a newspaper, President Lincoln wrote: "My paramount object in this struggle is to save the Union, and is not either to save or to destroy slavery. What I do about

slavery and the colored race, I do because I believe it will help save the Union."[1]

Fort Sumter

Less than one month after Lincoln became president, the Civil War broke out. On April 12, 1861, the Confederate Army attacked Fort Sumter in Charleston Harbor, South Carolina. The bombardment continued for thirty-six hours. Lincoln called for 75,000 volunteers from the North to defend the Union. But he did not wait for Congress's approval. As a result, four more states seceded to

Jefferson Davis became the first, and only, president of the Confederate States of America on February 22, 1862.

join the Confederacy—Virginia, Arkansas, North Carolina, and Tennessee. Richmond, Virginia, became the Confederacy's new capital. The nation had split in two; the North and the South were at war.

First Battle of Bull Run

Soldiers on both sides were sure they would win in a few weeks. The first major battle was at Bull Run, near Manassas, Virginia, on July 21, 1861. No one expected the fighting to last long. Spectators from Washington even brought picnic baskets and

Did You Know?
uring the Civil War the North
sed hot-air balloons to spy on
he South.

Robert E. Lee became one of the South's best generals during the Civil War.

binoculars to watch. Thirty-five thousand Union troops fought against 25,000 Virginia soldiers. The Confederate army humiliated the North. Both sides now realized that the war would be long.

Battle of Antietam Creek

During the first year of the war, the Confederates won many victories as battles raged across the South, especially in Virginia. Lincoln decided it was time to change the purpose of the war. He saw that freeing the slaves was "essential to the preservation of the Union."[2]

Lincoln needed a Union victory. His Cabinet, Congress, and the press

The Confederate Army attacked Fort Sumter as ships tried to bring food and provisions to the U.S. soldiers there.

32

criticized the way he handled the war. His army struggled with eight different generals he hired and fired.

The Confederates were led by Robert E. Lee, a brilliant general. Lee hoped for a quick victory that would force the North to surrender. He invaded Maryland at a little stream called Antietam, on September 17, 1862. But the battle ended with Lee pulling back to Virginia. This would be the bloodiest single day of the war with 24,000 men killed or wounded. The war was not over, but more believed the North would win.

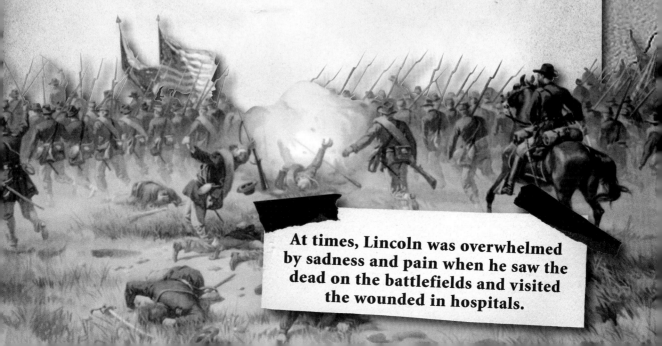

At times, Lincoln was overwhelmed by sadness and pain when he saw the dead on the battlefields and visited the wounded in hospitals.

EMANCIPATION PROCLAMATION

Chapter 8

Antietam was the long-awaited battle that proved that the North could hold its own against the South. Although it was not a victory, it allowed Lincoln to announce his plans. On September 22, 1862, the president issued this warning to the Confederate states: return to the Union by January 1, 1863, or I will free your slaves.

It was a courageous move that changed the course of the war and the nation. It was no longer a

This is the inkwell that Lincoln used to write the Emancipation Proclamation.

war to save the Union. It now became a war to free the slaves forever.

No states returned to the Union. So on New Year's Day, January 1, 1863, Lincoln issued the Emancipation Proclamation. Emancipation means freedom, and a proclamation is an announcement. It said that all slaves in the Confederate States of America "are, and henceforward shall be, free."

As he signed the document, Lincoln said:

The Emancipation Proclamation declared that slaves in the Confederate states would be "forever free."

If my name ever goes into history it will be for this act, and my whole soul is in it. If my hand trembles when I sign the Proclamation, all who examine the document hereafter will say, "He hesitated."[1]

Lincoln Links to Today

Lincoln laid the groundwork for three amendments to the Constitution that increased the rights of African Americans. In December 1865, Congress ratified the Thirteenth Amendment, which abolished slavery in the entire United States. The Fourteenth Amendment, adopted in 1868, gave all Americans— including African Americans— the right to "equal protection of the laws." The Fifteenth Amendment, passed in 1870, guaranteed black men (including former slaves) the right to vote.

In the meantime, the war raged on for two more years.

Slavery did not end in 1865. Today it still can be found in some countries, even though it is illegal under international law.

Lincoln surrounded himself with the brightest people. He filled his Cabinet with some of his greatest political rivals.

Lincoln Links to Today

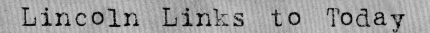

One hundred years after Lincoln signed the Emancipation Proclamation, blacks still did not have the same equal rights as whites. In the 1950s, the civil rights movement tried a new way to end segregation and to gain equal rights.

In 1963, Dr. Martin Luther King, Jr., organized a march on Washington, D.C., that attracted hundreds of thousands of supporters. Dr. King stood on the steps of the Lincoln Memorial and described a future in which all races would live together in peace and harmony. He challenged the nation in a speech that came to be known as "I Have a Dream".

The following year Congress passed the Civil Rights Act of 1964, which made segregation illegal. Today civil rights workers still continue to work for social change to improve society. They work on issues such as equal education and racial tolerance.

37

GETTYSBURG

In the quiet, peaceful little town of Gettysburg in Pennsylvania, the most important battle of the war was fought. It began on a hot day, July 1, 1863. It ended in horror three days later.

Robert E. Lee led his troops across Maryland and into Pennsylvania. General George G. Meade, the new Union general, rushed his army to fight Lee. The fighting was intense. Lee lost one-third of his army. It was a major defeat for the South; their last

Beginning of the earliest-known draft of the Gettysburg Address

39

attempt to invade the North had failed. When it ended, both sides saw more than seven thousand soldiers killed and another forty thousand wounded.

Lincoln Links to Today

When Lincoln was president he suspended civil liberties. He had arrested civilians in the North who protested the war. He said it was for national security. These suspected political criminals were tried in military courts.

There has always been an issue of national security versus civil liberties. After the September 11, 2001, attack on the United States, President George W. Bush used military courts to try suspected terrorists. He was criticized by some people for those actions.

Lee's army limped back to Virginia. On July 4, upon hearing the news of the Union's success, a very relieved Lincoln exclaimed, "I cannot, in words, tell you my joy over this result. It is great . . . it is great."[1]

Four Score and Seven Years Ago

In an attempt to honor the thousands of soldiers who died there, the battlefield at Gettysburg was dedicated as a national cemetery five months later, on November 19, 1863.

President Lincoln, one of the guest speakers, delivered a short speech which came to be known as the Gettysburg Address. It was only ten lines long, with 271 words that Lincoln had carefully chosen, and lasted only three minutes. But people there heard one of the most famous speeches in American history.

Lincoln began: "Four score and seven years ago . . ."[2] The beauty of the speech is that he used simple words to explain why the nation had to fight a cruel war. It showed his personal values as well as his views on democracy.

Gettysburg is a very popular site for people to visit.

THE GETTYSBURG ADDRESS

"Four score and seven years ago our fathers brought forth on this continent, a new nation, conceived in Liberty, and dedicated to the proposition that all men are created equal.

"Now we are engaged in a great civil war, testing whether that nation, or any nation so conceived and so dedicated, can long endure. We are met on a great battle-field of that war. We have come to dedicate a portion of that field, as a final resting place for those who here gave their lives that that nation might live. It is altogether fitting and proper that we should do this.

"But, in a larger sense, we can not dedicate—we can not consecrate—we can not hallow—this ground. The brave men, living and dead, who struggled here, have consecrated it, far above our poor power to add or detract. The world will little note, nor long remember what we say here, but it can never forget what they did here. It is for us the living, rather, to be dedicated here to the unfinished work which they who fought here have thus far so nobly advanced. It is rather for us to be here dedicated to the great task remaining before us—that from these honored dead we take increased devotion to that cause for which they gave the last full measure of devotion—that we here highly resolve that these dead shall not have died in vain—that this nation, under God, shall have a new birth of freedom—and that government of the people, by the people, for the people, shall not perish from the earth."[3]

POTUS, AGAIN

President Lincoln was at the lowest point of his political career during the summer of 1864. The war raged on and everyone held Lincoln responsible.

In spite of these pressures, he ran for re-election saying, "I want to finish this job of putting down the rebellion, and restoring peace and prosperity to the country."[1] His opponent was George B. McClellan, his former general who promised to put a quick end to the war.

The campaign became vicious. Even Lincoln did not believe he would win. "This morning as for some days past," he wrote, "it seems exceedingly probable that this Administration will not be re-elected."[2]

March to the Sea

Earlier in 1864, Lincoln had finally appointed a commander who would end the war no matter what the cost. Ulysses S. Grant believed in total war: strike at the enemy as hard and as often as you can. Grant planned a cruel scheme called the March to the Sea. He ordered General William T. Sherman to march his troops from Tennessee across Georgia to the Atlantic Ocean. They destroyed everything along the way that would help the enemy. Sherman's troops invaded Atlanta and burned it to the ground. The fall of Atlanta two months

Richmond, Virginia, the capital of the Confederate States of America, was destroyed as Union soldiers captured the city.

before election day was a major victory that helped Lincoln stay in office.

"With Charity for All"

As the North began to win battles, the mood of the country began to change. Lincoln was re-elected on November 8, 1864. His vice president was Senator Andrew Johnson, from Tennessee.

Lincoln was sworn in on the morning of March 4, 1865. Fifty thousand citizens gathered in the rain at the Capitol to hear him.

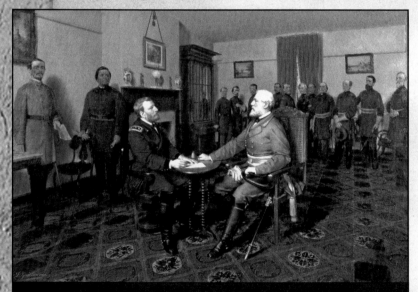

Robert E. Lee and Ulysses S. Grant discussed the terms of the Confederate Army of Northern Virginia's surrender in the town of Appomattox Court House at the home of Wilmer and Virginia McLean.

His speech did not boast of Union victories, but showed the forgiving side of this man. He spoke about reuniting the nation. He ended with a call to treat the South "with malice [ill will] toward none, with charity for all . . . to bind up the nation's wounds . . . to do all which may achieve and cherish a just, and a lasting peace, among ourselves, and with all nations."[3]

Surrender

On April 9, 1865, Lee was cornered. He surrendered his troops to Grant at Appomattox Court House, in Virginia. The war was finally over. The horrible cost of the war was more than half a million lives: approximately 360,000 Union soldiers and 260,000 Southern soldiers died. Most of the great cities of the South were destroyed.

Lincoln Links to Today

The President of the United States is the highest ranking officer in the armed forces. The Constitution gives this power to the president. But it also gives Congress the power to declare war.

Lincoln became a very active commander-in-chief as soon as the Civil War began. He increased the size of the army and navy. He spent millions of dollars without the approval of Congress. He blockaded Southern ports. He was criticized for these actions. But Lincoln believed the Constitution gave him this wartime power in order to protect the nation.

During times of war, other U.S. presidents have become active commanders-in-chief: Franklin D. Roosevelt during World War II, Lyndon B. Johnson during the Vietnam War, and George H. Bush during the Persian Gulf War.

Lincoln said the end of the war was the happiest day of his life. "Thank God I have lived to see this. I have been dreaming a horrid nightmare for four years and now the nightmare is over."[4]

Lincoln enjoyed only five days of peace before his life was taken from him.

FINAL HOURS

Chapter 11

Good Friday, April 14, 1865, was one of the happiest days of President Lincoln's life.[1] He had breakfast with his son Robert, who had just safely returned from battle. At 11 A.M. the president had his regular Friday Cabinet meeting. "Didn't our Chief look grand today?" one of them asked.[2] Lincoln was cheerful, a sharp contrast to the look of deep sadness and exhaustion that the burdens of war had etched on his face. Eating an apple, he returned to his office to greet visitors and sign papers.

At three o'clock he took a carriage ride with Mrs. Lincoln. She remembered: "During the drive he was so gay, that I said to him, laughingly, 'Dear

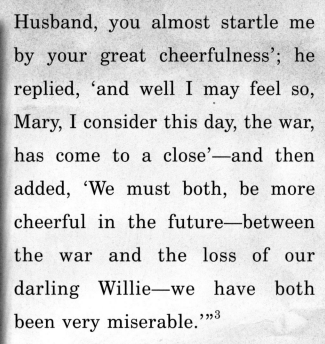

Did You Know?

Before his death, Lincoln had a dream. "There seemed to be a death-like stillness about me," he told a friend. "Then I heard subdued sobs, as if a number of people were weeping. . . . 'Who is dead in the White House?' I demanded of one of the soldiers. 'The President,' was his answer; 'he was killed by an assassin!'"[6]

Husband, you almost startle me by your great cheerfulness'; he replied, 'and well I may feel so, Mary, I consider this day, the war, has come to a close'—and then added, 'We must both, be more cheerful in the future—between the war and the loss of our darling Willie—we have both been very miserable.'"[3]

They had an early dinner and after eight o'clock drove by carriage to Ford's Theatre to enjoy a comedy, *Our American Cousin*. His advisers warned him not to go. There had been death threats against his life almost from the day he had been elected president.

The audience was cheering wildly as the President and Mrs. Lincoln entered the president's box. During the performance Mrs. Lincoln leaned closer to her husband and whispered, "What will [our guest] Miss Harris think of my hanging on to you so?" Smiling, Lincoln replied: "She won't think any thing about it."[4] Those were his last words.

Shortly after ten o'clock, a well-known twenty-six-year-old actor named John Wilkes Booth snuck into the president's box.

John Wilkes Booth was a well-known actor.

The gun that Booth used to assassinate President Lincoln is on display in the Ford's Theatre Museum, in Washington, D.C.

Booth was a fanatic of the Confederacy and simply hated Lincoln. He pulled out a pistol, leveled it two feet from the back of the president's head, and pulled the trigger. The sound of the shot was almost muffled by the audience laughing at the play. Booth leaped to the stage, yelling "Sic semper tyrannis," which means "thus always to tyrants"—the motto of Virginia. He fled from the theater. Mary Lincoln screamed, "They have shot the President! They have shot the President!"[5]

Lincoln was carried across the street to a boarding house and laid on a bed. His family and friends kept vigil. The sound of Mrs. Lincoln's sobs filled the house. Lincoln died the next day at 7:22 A.M. He was fifty-six years old. One of his Cabinet members quietly said, "Now he belongs to the ages."[7]

AN UNCOMMON MAN

Chapter 12

Within days of his death, the nation began to mourn President Lincoln as a great martyr who gave up his life for his country. In people's memories, Lincoln became larger and stronger and wiser than he was during his actual lifetime.

The Civil War showed his greatness as a leader, thinker, writer, and speaker. While dealing with the war, Lincoln also had to address other issues during his four years in the White House. He signed the Homestead Act in 1862, which gave 160 acres of free land to pioneer families who wanted to improve their lives.

This version of the Lincoln penny was first minted in 1959 in honor of Lincoln's 150th birthday.

This helped settle and develop the American West. He signed the Morrill Act of 1862 into law to create land-grant schools that later became state universities. This helped people from ordinary backgrounds like his create better lives for themselves. In 1862, Lincoln, who grew up on farms, created the Department of Agriculture to distribute seeds and agricultural information. Most Union families earned their income from farming at that time.

It took an extraordinary leader to accomplish all that Lincoln did. Some historians say he was a political genius who created the modern pres- idency. Besides wisdom, he had compassion, kindness, honesty, and humility,

The five dollar bill, like the penny, has Abraham Lincoln on the front and the Lincoln Memorial on the back.

and was able to rise above pettiness. These qualities helped him form friendships with people who opposed him. Lincoln faced his mistakes with honesty and shared credit for his successes.[1]

Lincoln lived the American dream. He was a common person who became uncommon.[2]

When he was twenty-three years old Lincoln wrote: "I have no other [ambition] so great as that of being truly esteemed of my fellow men, by rendering myself worthy of their esteem. How far I shall succeed in gratifying this ambition, is yet to be developed."[3]

A Voice Forever

Abraham Lincoln has a special place in our history. He is a symbol for national unity and

Did You Know?

Along with everything else he had accomplished, in the middle of the war in 1863, President Lincoln issued an order that created a national Thanksgiving Day. He wrote: "I do therefore invite my fellow citizens...to set apart and observe the last Thursday of November next, as a day of Thanksgiving and Praise ..."[4] Thanksgiving has been celebrated on that day ever since.

55

greatness. His qualities are the same ones that many believe are the best about America.

Lincoln speaks to all of us today through his powerful speeches and writings. He delivered a message to the U.S. Congress in December of 1862 that can guide the nation today:

> "Fellow-citizens, we can not escape history. . . . We . . . will be remembered in spite of ourselves. No personal significance or insignificance can spare one or another of us. . . . We, even we here, hold the power and bear the responsibility. . . . We shall nobly save or meanly [humbly] lose the last best hope of Earth."[4]

Chapter Notes

From "Fool" to Hero

1. Frank J. Williams, *Judging Lincoln* (Carbondale and Edwardsville, IL: Southern Illinois University Press, 2002), p. 3.

Chapter 1: The Making of a President

1. David H. Donald, *Lincoln* (New York: Simon & Schuster, 1995), p. 23.
2. Ibid., p. 28.
3. Doris Kearns Goodwin, *Team of Rivals* (New York: Simon & Schuster, 2005), p. 49.

Chapter 2: "Honest Abe"

1. "Excerpt of Abraham Lincoln's Letter to Martin M. Morris, March 26, 1843." *Lincoln/Net: Northern Illinois University.* 2000. http://lincoln.lib.niu.edu/teachers/religion-lincolnletter.html
2. David H. Donald, *Lincoln* (New York: Simon & Schuster, 1995), p. 44.
3. Doris Kearns Goodwin, *Team of Rivals* (New York: Simon & Schuster, 2005), p. 54.

Chapter 3: Marrying Miss Mary

1. Doris Kearns Goodwin, *Team of Rivals* (New York: Simon & Schuster, 2005), p. 200B.
2. David H. Donald, *Lincoln* (New York: Simon & Schuster, 1995), p. 85.

Chapter 4: A Rising Star

1. "House Divided Speech," *Abraham Lincoln Bicentennial 2009: About Lincoln.* http://www.lincolnbicentennial.gov/about/speeches/housedivided.php

Chapter 5: Slavery

1. Doris Kearns Goodwin, *Team of Rivals* (New York: Simon & Schuster, 2005), p. 190.

2. Ibid, p. 228.

Chapter 6: Hail to the Chief

1. "Farewell Address," *Abraham Lincoln Bicentennial 2009: About Lincoln.* http://www.lincolnbicentennial.gov/about/speeches/farewelladdress.php

2. "First Inaugural Address," *Abraham Lincoln Bicentennial 2009: About Lincoln.* http://www.lincolnbicentennial.gov/about/speeches/first inaugural.php

Chapter 7: Mr. Lincoln's War

1. Stephen B. Oates, *With Malice Toward None* (New York: Harper and Row, 1977), p. 313.

2. "Lincoln," *National Park Service; Abraham Lincoln Birthplace National Historic Site,* http://www.nps.gov/abli/parknews/frequently-asked-questions.htm

Chapter 8: Emancipation Proclamation

1. Doris Kearns Goodwin, *Team of Rivals* (New York: Simon & Schuster, 2005), p. 499.

Chapter 9: Gettysburg

1. David H. Donald, *Lincoln* (New York: Simon & Schuster, 1995), p. 446.

2. "Gettysburg Address," *Abraham Lincoln Bicentennial 2009: About Lincoln.* http://www.lincolnbicentennial.gov/about/speeches/gettysburg.php

3. Ibid.

Chapter 10: POTUS, Again

1. Doris Kearns Goodwin, *Team of Rivals* (New York: Simon & Schuster, 2005), p. 648.

2. Ibid.

3. "Second Inaugural Address," *Abraham Lincoln Bicentennial Commission 2009: About Lincoln.* http://www.lincolnbicentennial.gov/about/speeches/secondinaugural.php

4. Goodwin, p. 716.

Chapter 11: Final Hours

1. Doris Kearns Goodwin, *Team of Rivals* (New York: Simon & Schuster, 2005), p. 731.

2. Ibid., p. 732.

3. Ibid., p. 733.

4. Stephen B. Oates, *With Malice Toward None* (New York: Harper and Row, 1977), p. 431.

5. David H. Donald, *Lincoln* (New York: Simon & Schuster, 1995), p. 597.

6. Donald, p. 599.

7. Oates, pp. 425-426.

Chapter 12: An Uncommon Man

1. Doris Kearns Goodwin, *Team of Rivals* (New York: Simon & Schuster, 2005), pp. xvi-xvii.

2. Frank J. Williams, *Judging Lincoln* (Carbondale and Edwardsville, IL: Southern Illinois University Press, 2002), p. 15.

3. Goodwin, p. 87.

4. "Proclamation of Thanksgiving," *Abraham Lincoln Online: Speeches & Writings.* http://showcase.netins.net/web/creative/lincoln/speeches/thanks.htm

5. "Abraham Lincoln's Annual Message to Congress—Concluding Remarks," *Abraham Lincoln Online: Speeches & Writings.* http://showcase.netins.net/web/creative/lincoln/speeches/congress.htm

Glossary

abolitionist—A person opposed to slavery.

amendment—A change to the United States Constitution.

assassinate—To murder an important person, usually a political person.

civil war—A war that is fought between people of the same nation.

Confederate States of America—The eleven southern states that left the United States of America between 1861 and 1865, in hopes of becoming a new, separate nation: Alabama, Arkansas, Florida, Georgia, Louisiana, Mississippi, North Carolina, South Carolina, Tennessee, Texas, and Virginia.

democracy—A system of government in which power belongs to the people, who rule either directly or through elected representatives.

emancipation—Freedom, such as from slavery.

Emancipation Proclamation—An announcement made by President Abraham Lincoln that freed the slaves in the confederate states.

Fifteenth Amendment—A Constitutional Amendment passed in 1870 that granted the right to vote to all men, regardless of race.

Fourteenth Amendment—A Constitutional Amendment adopted in 1868 that granted equal protection to all citizens.

Homestead Act—A law passed by Congress in 1862 that gave 160 acres of public land to any head of a family who paid a fee, built a house, and worked the land for at least five years.

martyr—A person who suffers or is killed because of his or her beliefs.

proclamation—An announcement.

secede—To break away from.

segregation—A policy of separating people according to race in public areas, such as schools.

Thirteenth Amendment—A Constitutional Amendment adopted in 1865 that abolished slavery.

Further Reading

Books

Deutsch, Stacia and Rody Cohen. *Blast to the Past: Lincoln's Legacy.* New York: Simon & Schuster, 2005.

Hale, Sarah Elder, ed. *Cobblestone - The Civil War: Abraham Lincoln, Defender of the Union.* Peterborough, NH: Cobblestone Publishing, 2005.

Stone, Tanya Lee. *Abraham Lincoln.* New York: DK Publishing, 2005.

Internet Addresses

Abraham Lincoln Bicentennial
http://www.lincolnbicentennial.gov

Abraham Lincoln Birthplace National Historic Site
http://www.nps.gov/abli/parknews/frequently-asked-questions.htm

Abraham Lincoln Online: Speeches & Writings
http://showcase.netins.net/web/creative/lincoln/speeches/speeches.htm

Index

A

abolitionists, 21, 22, 24
Atlanta, Georgia, 45

B

battles,
    Antietam Creek, 32–33
    Appomattox Court House, 47
    Bull Run, 31–32
    Fort Sumter, 30
    Gettysburg, 39–40
Berry, William, 9–10
Black Hawk War, 8–9
Booth, John Wilkes, 51–52
Brown, John, 23–24
Bush, George H., 48
Bush, George W., 40

C

Civil Rights Act of 1964, 37
Civil War, 4, 30–33, 34–35, 39–41, 45–48
Confederate Army, 30, 32–33
Confederate States of America, 29, 34, 35
Congress, 17, 30, 32, 36, 37, 48, 56
Constitution, 22, 36, 48

D

Declaration of Independence, 22
Democrat, 19
Department of Agriculture, 54
Douglas, Stephen A., 18–19
Dred Scott v. Sanford, 22

E

Emancipation Proclamation, 35, 37

F

Fifteenth Amendment, 36
Ford's Theatre, 50
Fourteenth Amendment, 36

G

Georgia, 29, 45
Gettysburg Address, 41, 42
Grant, Ulysses S., 45, 47

H

Hamlin, Hannibal, 26
Herndon, William, 17
Homestead Act of 1862, 53

J

Johnson, Andrew, 46
Johnson, Lyndon B., 48
Johnston, Sarah Bush (stepmother), 6

K

King, Jr., Dr. Martin Luther, 37
Knob Creek, 5

L

Lee, Robert E., 33, 39, 40, 47
Lincoln, Abraham,
    adult, 8–11, 17–19